MW01592622

Aleph, broken

Poems from My Diaspora

For Karen —
The joys of language
Judy

Aleph, broken

Poems from My Diaspora

Judith Kerman

BROADSTONE

© 2016 by Judith Kerman
All rights reserved.
First edition.

Library of Congress Control Number 2015956663

ISBN 978-1-937968-22-9

Cover and Interior Design by Laurie Powers
Fonts used in this book are Cambria and Trebuchet

Author photograph copyright © 2014 by Franco Vogt

    The author wishes to thank the following publications in which
many of the poems in this collection previously appeared, sometimes
in different form: *The Bloomsbury Anthology of Contemporary Jewish
American Poetry* (Bloomsbury), *Cezanne's Carrot, Comstock Review,
Driftwood Review, Earth's Daughters, Galvanic Response* (March Street
Press), *Garfield Review, Jews., Jewish Currents, World to Come: Jewish
Currents 2015 Anthology, The Journal of Feminist Studies in Religion,
Mad Hatter's Review, The MacGuffin, Nature in Literature and Society,
Poemeleon, Poetry in Michigan / Michigan in Poetry* (New Issues Press),
Postcards from America (Post Traumatic Press), *Pudding, A Slant of Light*
(Codhill Press), *Umbrella,* and *Union: Jewish Currents 2014 anthology.*

Broadstone Books
An Imprint of
Broadstone Media LLC
418 Ann Street
Frankfort, KY 40601-1929

BroadstoneBooks.com

CONTENTS

III. Global Positioning

Liminal: After the Funeral

A book tells secrets
it's dying to share
once the mourning ends.
Some pages inked, others blank.
Like the rest of the world
the blank ones struggle
to rid themselves of purity.
Fire eats the pages
and I hear the whisper
of sleet hitting branches.
I don't need anyone's permission
to tell the story.

I. Conundrum

Cholent

The tradition is a stone building
windows filled with yellow light.
Black letters, square and mysterious as granite.
Wrought iron, that other voice:
Arbeit Macht Frei
spreading its arms across the gate.
The sword turns at the door.

I sit by Grandpa,
a wriggling toddler,
the only female in the *shul*.
I do not see a balcony, a curtain
hiding the women.
Old men in black fedoras
bow and sing.
The echo of the flames
is close in our ears; I do not know
the names of Grandpa's brothers
who died before I was born.

Fridays, women in other houses
rush about, cleaning and cooking,
heating the oven to keep the *cholent* hot—
meat and fruit, a stewing sweetness
I've never tasted.
My mother didn't stand
white cloth on her head
lighting candles.
At Chanukkah, when I put the menorah
in the window, I hear the glass breaking.

Those who understand these images...
Those who don't...

The books open the wrong way.
Yellow light
lies under the apple trees
like honey.

Millefiore

I coveted Grandpa's paperweight,
a big old millefiore,
all through my childhood.
Huge and heavy,
concentric honeycomb
of glass flowers in a crystal sphere.

Later, I gave my father
art-glass paperweights
so I could always find
a gift for him:
a speckled white orb
with markings like petroglyphs,
a tear-drop shape
flashing iridescence,
a sand dollar
fossilized to gleaming pyrite.
He always said, "I don't need it,"
a line he inherited from Grandpa.
But of course it
missed the point.

My father, at twelve, had a revelation:
there is no God.
He refused to be *bar mitzvah*.
No one has ever talked
about the fight they must have had.
He gave that gift to me.
When Grandpa died,
I was nineteen.
The next day, I came down
with German measles. All week,
I curled up under the flower quilt
reading *Lord of the Rings*,
spared having to sit *shiva*.

From *Pictures at an Exhibition*

Two Jews argue on a street
in Eastern Europe, late nineteenth
century. Soot and grit, stone
buildings. Draft horses haul
wagons along the cobbled streets.
Somewhere nearby, my grandfather
is helping to print pamphlets
and dreaming of revolution. Last year,
he quit *yeshiva*, and he's still arguing
with his father who prefers not to make
trouble. In Moussourgsky's music the big
pompous left hand of the piano
talks down to the little skinny
tinkling keys—in Ravel's familiar
orchestration, low strings
and muted trumpet, a *klezmer* voice.
The big man has a white silk
cravat, a black homburg, velvet
lapels. The little one has holes
in his shoes, frayed cuffs on a threadbare
jacket. My grandfather is afraid
that he'll be drafted, sent away
for 30 years of hard labor
and anti-Semitic harassment. He'd
rather go to jail. Moussourgsky
thinks they're funny, these two,
the one who thinks he has power, the one
who doesn't.

Stories

for my father

that sharp-edged gravel caught in your throat
you pursed your mouth
old raptor
sitting up in bed
talking to the surgeon from behind
your *New York Times*
as if you didn't care

*

I never told you
about the owl I once found on a country road
I spread its wings, soft and huge
in my hands, a bronze and ivory fan
closed its dark eyes
and felt the small skull
through a crown of stiff feathers
it's buried in my back garden

*

at a party once, you said that
Grandpa hid in a water tower
while peasants burned the town
my brother and I had to imagine
the details
I once found the letters
you wrote to Mom from Saipan
when you were in the Army
but I didn't read them

*

when I asked you to write your memoirs
you said you were left back
in first grade
just off the boat from Poland
but by the second year, you said
you could speak English

Snapshot

It's somewhere in Europe—
Poland or Germany,
you can tell by the buildings.
The two of them look
so carefree, but it's hard to say
who they are:
newlyweds, good friends on holiday.
The picture is blurry, as if
floating underwater.
I don't know if they were
relatives of mine.
But I feel drawn in
to that city square,
the old buildings squatting
stolid as *burgomeisters*,
where people are hiding
in cellars filled with fine old wines.
My mouth waters
at the memory of *konditorei*
with their chocolate-wrapped marzipan balls.
In American, we have no equivalent
to *gemütlichkeit*.
Or the white sausages,
tasty but slightly obscene,
the white asparagus
picked before the sun got to it.

Aleph, broken

for my unknown ancestors

slides from her
warm soup into bitter air,
breathes but does not cry,
the start
of a life without promises,
the dirty floor where language
will creep but no one hears it.
She is the first child.
Describe poverty.
Describe the ache to say.

When she is old enough
to read, the letters crack
and fall apart, flakes of burnt paper.
She is a window with a missing pane.
Wind blows through on winter nights.
Her father's hat and beard
hunch over the kitchen table,
a shawl over his shoulders,
his hand trembling with chill
as he traces the lines of text.

Learning Haftorah

Hooks of letters
tangle and unwind; ancient music
groans in a boy's ear.
Why should he give up
the sunlight?
Sixty years ago
when the teacher was a boy
telegrams arrived from Europe.
There was nothing he could do
but study, draftee
in a war against forgetting.
The child he teaches
resents the sacrifice
but he's a good boy.
He comes and works,
watches the teacher's knobby finger
move across the page.
Sometimes, he thinks he hears
the old voices, even at home,
the book on his desk jammed
at an angle between his math text
and his soccer ball,
the drone of a mosquito
he tries to brush away.

Poem for the name Bess

for my mother

Absence. The whisper
of a cat brushing past the sofa leg,
whiskers bristling. Paintings
behind their glass, done
when I was a baby:
green and brown trees
in a triangular park,
blurred figures on benches,
a blue hat, a dot of red.
The bridge swagging its lights
across blue evening,
the view I saw
snuggled in your arms
looking out the window over rooftops.

Conversation

You're hard, she says. I think maybe she's right. What can I do
with her pain? The Lone Ranger comes rushing up on his silver
steed, but that's not right. I don't know how to comfort, only how
to solve. Salve is not the same word. Dissolve. I cradle the new
scar forming on my belly where there will not be a child, as there
could no longer be a child for a decade now. A cantaloupe cut
open. A railroad track where I stand looking down the vanishing
perspective and no train is coming, ever. My mother hurts, has
strange ailments the doctors can't diagnose, or maybe they're
tired of frail old ladies. I don't want her to hurt, but there's
nothing I can do. It's a shell, Mother, a protection for my own
pain. Or against it. When I knock, I hear the echo of nothing there.

Conundrum

— noun —

1: a riddle
How can it be
that the self evaporates,
rising like a wisp of steam off the body,
diffused into air?
One moment, a pudgy two-year-old,
I respond, laughing, to my young mother,
lovely in her high cheekbones and auburn hair.
The next, there is no one there.

2: a question or problem having only a conjectural answer
You need to interview the old folks.
I recall tying saddle-shoes,
their white chalked with polish but still smudged,
the back seat of the old black Studebaker,
falling down stairs,
dreaming of falling down stairs.
Too late now
to ask what they remembered:
Daddy working in the family store after school,
Mom and her aunt, new immigrants.
smiling at the camera,
squinting into the autumn sun.

3: an intricate and difficult problem
Someone is required to identify
the body before burial,
the *golem* without the sacred Name.
In the open coffin, red lipstick my mother
might have worn, white hair sprayed stiff
as she would never do,
only the bones of her face
perhaps familiar.

Ambivalence

1) You have to treat udder in a special way
   before it is eaten
   to remove the milk.
   Like blood in the liver.

2) Or maybe cook it in a special pot
   udderly dedicated.

3) Or maybe since it's flesh
   the milk squeezed from it
   is flesh too.
   Theoretically, you could make
   fleischig cheese.

4) Blood is allowed
   straight from the wound
   though prohibited drunk from a cup.
   So you may suck a cut finger.

5) Human breastmilk is *pareve*,
   the opposite *halacha*
   from blood.
   It goes with anything.
   You can drink it in a cup
   but not straight from the body
   once you've been weaned.

6) Yalta taught, for everything prohibited there
   is something similar permitted.

Parable

Small
green
apples
fall on the
ground around the tree,
hard enough to bruise. Something soft
appears where soil and apple kiss: rot begins to stain
the metal with something the color of blood, sweetness.

White Light

I remember him, one day,
pretending to read the paper
with just his clip-on sunglasses
balanced on his nose.

My mother
washed out his soiled pajamas.
He couldn't get up,
wouldn't get up:
round-shouldered,
pot-bellied,
his big hard head,
his voice like sandpaper
wheezing, hands shaking.

Now white light
floods in through the window,
an empty recliner
with oily stains
where his head rested
when he napped.
Grey tinges the armrest covers
though my mother
washed them weekly.

Grief

—noun—

1. Heavenly effort. When the sun rises, you will know what to do next. For now, try to sleep.

2. Sweet prickling at the ends of branches, noses turned into the warming air.

3. Searching. A long wait by a phone that does not ring.

Metaphysics

for my father

The rabbi asked,
he wasn't really an atheist
was he? More of an
agnostic? But you
imagined the universe
mechanical. I don't know
if that meant gears. Perhaps
atomic nuclei. When I said
the world is a living being
you called me Pantheist,
an affectionate insult.
We never talked
metaphor, although I probably
learned it from you.
What is left then
under the flat lawn with its sprinklers
under the sandy soil
in the concrete vault
in the wooden casket
in your good sports jacket
in the skin bag
among the suppurating microbes?
You are gone beyond
the blank black door.
That's all
anyone can say.

The Use of Force in Public Architecture

Stalin was a builder,
stone and steel.
Hitler sat at his drafting board
trying to abandon Roman forms.
Coffins for mortar boxes,
bones for lime.

They drew new cities, railroads,
barracks and the round mouths of ovens,
watched the streetsweeper,
the greengrocer piling fruit at dawn.
They smelled the sweat of a ditchdigger
eating a garlic sandwich.
Wolves chewed the limbs
of the dead soldiers.

To build new cities,
the old must be demolished.
(Announced it on the radio;
marched it down the middle of the street.)
The citizens were happy; it was official.
They washed their faces at the public fountain.
They sat on commissions of inquiry.
One building remained standing.

At the Holocaust Museum

Prurient fingers catalog
the photographs:
rabbis, scholars, shopkeepers,
black coats and beards,
wives and children
huddled under kerchiefs.

Among them,
Polish peasants Jews still learn
to hate. Gypsies, homosexuals. Communists.
The Jews of the Enlightenment,
men who argued in coffeehouses,
founded newspapers,
resurrected Hebrew and imagined Zion
as socialism;
women who could read,
who ran stores
and raised literate children. Look
at those photographs, too—
double-breasted suits, cloche hats,
their European children glowing in lace dresses
before pastoral studio scrims.
Grief keeps its memories
in holes in the earth,
tin boxes eaten by the acid soil.
Humus and human, *adam v'adamah.*
Warehouses full of
hair weighed, teeth counted,
eyeglasses and valises,
the feedstock of factories, apparatus
of profit and loss.
Talismans: photos of corpses, of piles of shoes.
Today, the rabbis sponsor trips for teenagers.
Go to Israel, they say. Learn Hebrew.
It will answer all your questions.

Israel

—noun—

1. The national name of the Hebrew people; see also Jew, Israelite.

2. Dreaming.

3. Jacob after he dreamed.

4. An infected cut that pulls when I stretch, throbs at rest.

5. A settler state.

6. Where we will be safe if all else fails.

7. What I wrestle with.

8. Love and fear, meeting on a desert road and making peace.

9. The land belongs to No One. We walk on it and draw lines. *Mine!* we declare in that toddler voice.

11. Blood ties. And blood.

Pumpernickel

It came home with Daddy
on the train from New York,
round and heavy
with a hard mahogany crust,
knobbly as stone.
We ate it weekend mornings,
dense and chewy, mottled grey and tan,
sliced thin, with full-fat
Philadelphia cream cheese.

They offer bread like that
in Germany on hotel buffets,
not what they sell here,
flimsy and burnt-sugar black
or damp black bricks of
whole rye, imported.
Daddy insisted Stuhmer's used
no coloring, but I tried
whole wheat, rye meal, barley, buckwheat,
paged through recipes
flavored with cocoa, molasses, coffee
looking for that bitterness.

Online, you find a small universe
of people who remember
Stuhmer's pumpernickel.
Someone's posted a photo
of a 1920's Stuhmer's truck.
Rye starter foams in the refrigerator,
a responsibility,
like caring for a pet
or visiting a grave.

II. Vessels

Shekinah

The perceptible manifestation of God in the world; the female emanation; what abides with the exiled Children of Israel; that part of God in exile from Godhead, according to Kabbalist tradition, which human holiness helps to reconcile.

Indwelling
dwelling in
the body, as a house
as the world, dwelling
in the darkness
and the light which is darkness
the galaxy spreading in space and fire
the stars above the roof
going-in, ongoing
be here with us

indwelling
dwelling in
the body, as a house
in the world, dwelling

indwelling
dwelling in
the body, as a world
as a house, a tree
exploding with birds
in the darkness which is
light among exiles
the birds flying into windy sky
be here with us

indwelling
dwelling in
the world as a body
as a house
in the darkness which is
the light
we reach to touch you
be here with us
presentness, be here with us
here with us

Imagining Shabbat

Flowing away
flowing away
sand underfoot becomes hollow
as the wave ebbs
takes away
the ground under my feet

here, for a while
it might stop

Mehitzah

It's long and unfamiliar, the road
of returning to myself.

—*Angela Hernández*

I work at making it real,
asphalt with concrete curbs.
Sometimes I imagine my great grandparents
standing by the side.
His face is hidden by his black beard.
Hers is in shadow.
A burning *yahrtzeit* candle
sits on a shelf
in a kitchen miles away.

I walk past the blank-faced houses,
the stories of pogroms and wars,
the family history no one ever told.
No one has imagined
my life, a woman with no family to cook for,
no children to bless.
This is not a complaint.

My hands know more than I do,
touching old wine cups,
prayer shawls, braided bread.
I will not cover my hair.
I will not accept the *mehitzah*,
the seat in the balcony behind a screen.
A pair of candle flames
glows through the window.

A little at a time
I begin to read the old language,
though it is still an iron grate,
a bricked-up window.
When I put my ear to the wall,
I hear men's voices, a sobbing sound.

Heritage

The first time I met her
she was marrying my cousin,
but she said he was "different."
Sweet face and sugared condescension,
she thinks she's beyond the dirty collars
and mule dung of her people.
I hide from her
the one she would call
a "little Jew," my ancestor.
He wanted justice.
His passion reached above
the stink of stairwells
and leaky roofs,
bean soup in the anteroom,
gaslights glowing yellow
in the dust of old books.
He was an ordinary man,
ashes in his pocket.
He wanted to be Chosen.
People who, I imagine,
looked like her,
people who worshipped her martyred god
broke his bones
and raped his daughter.
I don't want to remember
how his shame
curled into a club:
"Better to burn the Torah
than teach it to women."
All my life I've run from him, from her.
I want to speak past it,
woman to woman,
but I don't know
what's possible between us.
She doesn't see me
for who I am.

A man at the *shul* tells me:
"What the *goyim* did to us,
who cares if she's offended!"

Algorithm

We now know that
there are no limits...
            —Daniel Landes

Everything is permitted,
even the end,
children starving
while the smell of sauerbraten
blows over barbed wire fences.
We like living well,
sensible burghers
asleep under a feather tick.
So we plan ahead.
We have a computer model
of the end;
we keep it on a shelf
between the Bible and *Das Kapital*.

The end is a recipe for potato soup,
one rotten spud to the gallon.
It glows in the dark
like the plastic keychain charm
of a skull
I had when I was twelve.

The purpose of the Revolution
is sleeping through the night.
I promise I will never
leave you alone,
shivering
in the roar of furnaces.

Imagining Sukkot

Your tents, O Yaacov...
            —Numbers 24:5

The children camped
across the desert 40 years
with never any rain to fall on them
holes in a roof
not solid anyway but thatched
with branches

the delusion that there could be
stone palaces
now the kids want to
put up a nylon tent
next to the barbecue
they giggle at crackling branches
the possum who lives
under the neighbor's shed
scuffles through the leaves
and stares, eyes glowing red
into the flashlight
starlight gleams through gaps
in the dark branches as suburbanites
try to sleep on an air mattress
on a pressure-treated deck
in the backyard of a house
the silence never absolute
the sound of freeway traffic
carried miles on the wind

once a year for a week
hoping it won't rain.

Ritual Bath

The *mikveh* should be
blue water reflecting open sky,
like floating in my mother,
perfect dependence.
Not this tiled room
entered by the rear door
near the dumpster.
Remember to breathe,
remember
the world outside
where sunlight has heated
the cistern on the rooftop
so this water is almost
too hot.
Duck my head seven times.
Affirm the skin I wear is
Jewish, always imagine
dark shadows below the surface,
piles of bones, piles of hair.
Duck my head seven times.
Let it all float away,
ocean roaring
in my ears...

Erev Yom Kippur

darkness shuttles across the sky
this is the night we sing
Kol Nidre, standing in the gateway
between the Torah scrolls
opened into terror

around the edges
possibility gleams
lightning hangs
from filaments of air
filled with light
with silica dust

hail pounds down
its white marbles and
onion layers
ask in advance
for forgiveness of our human
failures, slice back
the sting of tears

I refuse it

don't breathe
tree branches wrestle with storm wind
thunder rumbles under its breath
rain strikes our heads
the thin rods
of a lock slamming home

Before

One time
night fell
and kept on falling
there were stars
all over the ground
the earth began to burn.

All night birds flew
through a sky
with no stars
with light coming up
from below.

The birds got tired
and came down to find seeds
the stars were in their way
and burned their feet
a bird picked up a star
a seed of fire
it glowed like a gem
in the bird's beak
the sun came up
and splashed light on the stars
until they went out.

The sun went away
and it was dark again
with no stars
the birds sat on the ground
and waited.

Basya

The Rabbis called Pharoah's daughter
Basya, "God's daughter."

my mother
porcelain cup
a face of shadows
when you hold it up to light

her will strong
as wicker
or bridges built of toothpicks
strong enough to carry the weight
of a grown man

when my father died
she rowed her own boat
took on board
everything left behind

last year's nest
rocked dangerously
in the wind of an April storm
down plucked from the breast
and thin sticks

White Light Again

this is what I don't understand
this white light

a space where my lifetime of emotion
fizzles like a match dipped into water

at midnight I have the impulse
to call her as I used to

when I listen to my answering machine
her voice is not there

we should have kept recordings
those long conversations that wandered
through paths branching sideways

and when I said "I've got to go now, Mom"
she'd start a new topic

Album

Aunt Olga, in a white nightgown, brushes out her long dark hair. It reaches down past her waist. That white nightgown is the shirt in one of my poems.

The iron bed in Bubbe's house is so high above the floor that someone has to set me on it at bedtime. A headboard of vertical iron pipes connected to a round arch, painted white. As I fall asleep, the voices of grownups in another room.

Bubbe's millinery shop in the living room bay window, behind a room divider, has just enough space for a little work table and chair. A head-shaped stand holds a hand-made navy felt pillbox with a navy veil. Down below, beyond the sheer white curtains, traffic on Livingston Avenue.

The girl cousins write "stories" on slips of paper in an upstairs bedroom in Maplewood, my uncle and aunt's house. Then we tuck them into the tops of our stockings, run down two flights into the basement and burn them in the coal furnace so no one will see them.

A recurring dream of falling downstairs.

A thundercloud with bright sunlight around the edges. I remember it as a "silver lining."

A group of us, about 6 years old, pretend we can write script at a party at Grandma's house in the Bronx, curving lines and loops.

I watch Grandma rolling and cutting fresh noodles in her kitchen.

The grownups are arguing in another room. I can't make out the words, but Grandma's voice sounds like she is talking and crying at the same time.

Writing an Epitaph

On stone, words have a different energy.
Devoted husband and father. Dear friend, never to be forgotten.
His grave is still a turf rectangle, grass blades
just turning green, and a small plastic nameplate.
We walk among the graves,
reading. Granite,
some of it already beginning to weather. Bronze plaques.
This is an interfaith garden, some family stones
marked with both crosses and *magen davids*.
Stones are flush to the ground
so the lawn can be mowed.
Only a few go on at length,
like the love-letter from a bereaved husband
carved into a slab
the size of a twin bed. A ceramic photo
shows a luminous blonde in her 40s.
My mother knew sides of him
he never showed to anyone else. And in his last years,
he was already not quite there,
sinking slowly into the television set,
an accountant who made errors in his own tax returns.
We need a pun, since he loved them,
or a crossword puzzle,
a star for a Jewish atheist.

Consumerism: A Lecture

Two, and two,
and two,
and two. Task to task,
moment to hour to day.
Flashes of things
I need to remember. Ad-
ministration: Do I minister?
I think of death,
a blank wall of perplexity.
We eat the world, a metaphor
of fire, locust, blight, frost;
use it, and use it up,
leaving nothing behind, only
the tubercular bodies of things, objects,
goods. Trying to balance—what we sell
and what we are asked for.
Use is a form of borrowing,
permeable membrane,
imaginary line,
like profiles that look at the vase:
molecules of smog mutating in sunlight,
amino acids coupling in the primeval ocean.
The moth appears and disappears
in its camouflage.

The Assistant V.P.
Imagines Herself as a Butcher

In her business
blood is a commodity.
Beef sides dangle in the cooler;
knives and cleavers gleam.
Chuck. Rump. Sirloin.
When customers come in, the bell
tinkles over the door.

The smell of blood is neighborly:
two chops, a pound of ground round.
Her hands caress a shoulder of lamb,
sweetbreads, the clean strings of sausages.
She wraps filets in crisp brown paper.
A yellow cat wolfs his liver scraps
and sits down to wash in a sunny window.

It's cold work—
sometimes her hands ache.
At night she dreams
she is walking down a sidewalk
with the black-grey sheen of steel.
Dried hands dangle in shop windows.
She's hungry.

Vessels

Carrying a bowl of hot
soup across a wet tile floor
Climbing a ladder with a storm window
Dancing with someone new
Thinking of a dying friend

The Midrash says
there was an earlier creation

It did not hold

Perhaps there was too much
holiness
The harsh law, adamant
could not hold
The particles rushed
in every direction

Sitting alone in the dark
listen
Is the holy
everywhere?
How shall I see it?

The Midrash says
holy was everywhere
filling space and time
To make room for us
it withdrew
to make room for us

III. Global Positioning

Global Positioning

Rain outside
Light slides into the room
like the slime trail of the slugs
that eat holes in my tomatoes

The soft dapple
of a slug's mucous skin
shines as it glides
along the kitchen table
away from the basket

Where are you going
waving your knobbed antennae
You seem so sure
of your direction

Fragile

It is a large ceramic jar with a shiny glaze. Most of the surface is mottled turquoise, sometimes shading toward royal blue. Around the shoulders and forming the handles are gold dragons, bright metallic gold with curlicues and bosses, talons, fingers, tongues lapping at the blue water of the glaze.

If you look closely at the blue surfaces, you will see waves moving, the lines of surf, silent from this height; two people relaxing on a float near some rocks. A ship moves across the horizon, trailing a thread of smoke.

A gold dragon holds the sun in its mouth. If not for the dragon, the sun would be too strong, and the sea might boil away. The dragon protects us, as the Chinese have always taught. Its fierce love breathes out the atmosphere that we breathe in, the cool wind, the iodine and salt smell near the beach, the sound of breakers through an open window at night.

Salad

The cut side of a fresh tomato
gleams like the world
seen from space:
jeweled lights,
swirls of flesh
flow and ebb.
Salt floods the open places
where my heartbeat pauses,
and I might, if I choose,
plunge in,
splash in the juice,
swim to the horizon,
Red Sea unfurling,
opening its arms.

Bird of Paradise

The flame of a torch
bursts from its green pipe
here by the steps of my mother's
Florida condo. It pokes its orange beak

at the horizon, spikes
its yellow mohawk backward.
I want to believe
it's native,

but it's South African,
a gardener's fantasy
among the gargantuan pothos,
also immigrant,

"Devil's Ivy,"
climbing the palmettos.
Parrots squawk
in the strangler figs,

native, but invasive,
and the mockingbird
defies her plain grey feathers
in florid arias.

The early morning
breaks into leaf-blower roar,
Haitian workers wearing
hearing protectors,
riding lawn tractors
around sprinkler systems
that turn on in the rain.

Sibling Rivalry

My brother is standing under the ceiling fan
in my parents' Florida apartment,
turning a screwdriver with his left hand.
He holds the fan housing still
with his right.
For years I have been fascinated
by my brother's hands,
strong and muscular, but graceful.
I have hands
like my father's, with a square palm.
My brother's hands
are more beautiful than mine,
with longer fingers.

The postcard he once sent
is on my father's desk:
the temples of Bangkok
rising above the city streets
like glistening rooster-combs.
Taxi horns cry
Cock-a-doodle-do!
I ask my brother,
did you know that Thomas Merton died
in Bangkok when he stepped
out of the shower
and turned on an electric fan?

My brother says, I'd never
be stupid enough
to work on wiring with wet hands.

Saffron

the shirt I always imagine wearing—
not coral, not gold
but I can never quite
focus on the difference
fragrant rice smell
like that cinnamon and
turmeric stew (almost that
color)
Burmese monks' robes
"hot" sunset
tangerine
a glow, not salmon
like the light of October maples
reflecting off low clouds—
flames of the end of summer
hot hot hot
the fragrance of cinnamon, cumin
and onion
cream of tomato soup—too pastel
my frustrated efforts at color-mixing
wanting saturation, brilliance
paella in a Spanish café near the ocean
why not choose an easier color?
(I need an old
National Geographic)
no words for it—
not sweet, not hot
the glow persists

Penthouse View, Havana 2002

While the taxi waits,
I squint through the front door,
locked and derelict,
an elevator shaft yawning
through the dusty glass.
Around the back, in the alley,
I find rusted bells and a light,
a stairway almost too narrow for
two to squeeze past.
On a tiny landing between the floors,
doors to a small elevator.

No ceiling hatch.
For 13 unmarked floors
going up, going down
I crane my neck and watch
brick and cement pass by
like the inside of an unused chimney.
From the penthouse balcony
of the Residencia Académica,
only the sea, the sea wall
dotted sparsely with people sitting, talking,
looking outward.
Other concrete towers, most needing paint,
and the empty Malecón.
An occasional antique car
or bicycle or rattletrap Lada
passes down below.
Once, a new BMW
no Cuban could own.
13 stories up, the June wind
blows constantly,
warm and wet.

Fidel talks for hours
on the tube,
vigorous, but his voice

sounds his age.
The Assembly will confirm
socialism. Unanimously.
My President rattles the sword
and Fidel talks back.
His people are angry.
Patria o muerte,
they say.
Handsome and well-spoken teenagers,
men and women,
old, young and middle-aged,
black and white.
Patria o muerte.
A different kind of poetry.
Havana wilts,
hermosa y dilapidada,
a ghost city of old American cars,
rich people's houses
inherited by the poor
(like Detroit)
and tired, stubborn people.
The sea fills the view
from the penthouse,
from the Malecón,
spray coming over the seawall,
a few small boats bobbing,
and sometimes the heads of swimmers.

On Cubana de Aviación,
the flight attendants made announcements
in Spanish and English.
At the Assembly,
speakers call us *El Imperio.*
I think of *Star Wars* and its
storm trooper clones.
Everyone I know
who comes here

brings office supplies
and headache pills as gifts.
People beg in the street
for money and soap.
I give the children
ball-point pens.

Metáfora

—noun, Greek—

carriage, freightage,
traction, traffic
a sign on the side of
a moving van in Athens
beds, bureaus, boxes of books

the young tomcat
tracks birds in the branches
his haunches
prepare for launch

I fold and float
paper boats

Apocalypse

—noun—

1. The ruined temple of the goddess Calypso, once the center of her cult. Located at the highest point of the city Calypsos, of which she was patroness. Destroyed during a 50-year war with a neighboring city-state. The sun has blasted the bas-reliefs of her warrior kings.

2. A scrubby tree of semi-arid regions with grey-green foliage and a peculiar but pleasant pungency. Often used in dry flower arrangements. The main food of *ursus teddyus*, a small plush-furred quadruped. They sit in pairs among the branches, endlessly grooming each other.

3. A set of books containing names omitted or expunged from the New York Telephone Directory, held by certain groups to be the true record of the population. On sacred occasions, the names are read out in the city squares.

4. A type of speech impediment characterized by excessive sibilance. Thought to have been the sound made by certain ancient prophetesses when under the influence of their deity.

Third Red Car

The first silver casting I ever made,
a pendant, crescent moon crossed by a cloud,
looked more like a shark. My joke: the one who
knew what it was, he would be my one true
love. Like the servant by the city gate
waiting for Rebecca. Like standing at
the corner watching for the guy driving
the third red car. So do I believe in
fated love? I don't know, but I'm used to
being independent, and someone stole that
silver casting. Spinster is a word that
spits. But I still imagine I'll someday
meet the man who would see it right away:
a moon and a cloud, conjoined in the night sky.

The woman who buys her own diamonds

buys at auction
the auctioneer bawling his price his price
his prince
an antiques dealer
bidding against her from the back row

listens to the frogs chime
from a nearby marsh
but she's over forty

hopes but does not believe
does not take herself lightly

tilts the stones in sunlight, watches
the sparkles splash across her shirt
as she drives, ring hand on the wheel

wears it on her middle finger
so there's no mistake

Seeing My Heart

the mark of the ultrasound
hangs on the screen
like the light over a back door
in a night-time alley
where saxophone leaks from a corner bar
and glass shatters

the technician moves her sensor
plays my heart for me
in black and white
contingent music
the image shifts, dissolves
heart valves gleam
open their trumpet mouths

Sonata for Kitchen Table

solitary pedestal
wrought iron
and complicated
with cranks and set screws
a dream of the 19th century
a symphonic composition
wheels that score the flooring
with rust smudges
where the wash water
lingers in dents
in the vinyl
linoleum, asbestos tile
generations of flooring
under its wheels
a triumphal march
of domestic fashion
but without elephants
empty kitchen
I do not cook often
though I have a percussion section
pots
pressure cooker
wok
steel whip
Sabatier chef's knives
I don't know
how the top
got this gouge, although
I understand
wear, scars and wrinkles
the varnish
urethane, almost
down to the grain
of the old wood
the real ivory
piano keys

Surgical Scar

It looks like a southbound
railroad track, bending down the hill
and out of sight.

Weeds grow up
along the right of way.
Tramps walk the coarse gravel.

Hollowness rings underfoot
like stomping on hardpan
in a drought,

an echo of lost possibilities.
Her surgeon
gives her a photograph.

It looks like conjoined pears,
ripe and red.
She says, "I wasn't using it

for anything,"
makes jokes about
a valentine, a baby picture,

hanging around too much
with cats, who also have
a bicorn uterus.

Pathology reports a cyst,
a "wad" of blonde hair
and cells that could have

budded teeth.
Imaginary monsters.
On the phone, her cousin the oncologist

sounds impatient when she repeats
the folktale of absorbed twins.
He's heard it before.

Act IV

It's a comic opera
with a tragic ending.
The husky tabbycat
scarcely stirs the bare branches
of the bush he's under,
watching the squirrels with the intentness
of death coming. Their plush red tails
bob above the snow.
The jay screeches its alarm.
Later, the cat goes home
daintily across the snow
to purr around his owner's feet.
A nice cat.
Storm clouds filter sun
into moving shafts,
shadows on the horizon
like gates closing.

Hunting Season

Rain on the road,
smeared light
on the windshield,
prickling tension of
my shoulders
imagining a sniper,

spider-cracked
windshield, blown tire,
running off the shoulder.
Imagining the sniper's
malice, grinning to himself.

No patch on his shoulder.
He trained as a sniper, but this
is recreation, just for himself,
blood rush, speeding heartbeat.

I never used to imagine snipers,
never saw myself
a target. Even now my heartbeat
runs steady, watching for deer

at dusk. Not a hunter
myself, but my car
is a deadly weapon, steady beat
of windshield wipers, deer somewhere
out there, a risk in the dark.

Only these nights I imagine
the red bead of the laser pinning me
like a startled deer, the guy in camo
crouching in the dark
along the side of the road.

Tree Frog Ghazal

In May at dusk, white voices solo
in the swamp, thimble-sized frog sopranos.

On the first warm day, we take off our shoes.
Warm mud lushes up between our toes.

The cat in my arms chirps his purr, kneads,
pushes at my face with his leather nose.

Spring peepers chorus in the night,
sleighbells across moonlit snow.

We stroll past the factory. Light streams out, the din
of machinery tended by bleary men. Hot iron glows.

On the picket line, the men shouting
at young women wear lapel pins with 5 tiny toes.

How ignorant we are! I read, you study.
The world goes on beyond what anyone knows.

Crickets, caroling twists of wire, skitter
under dry leaves near the green tomatoes.

Frog larvae swimming in rain water
in the crotches of trees grow legs, then feet, then toes.

Judy, you say, come to bed.
We hold each other. The spinning earth slows.

Ice Fishing

In Michigan on winter nights,
lanterns scattered across the lakes
chip at the darkness.
Like fireflies, except the season's wrong.
As I drive the back roads,
clumps of trees break up the view:
an inlet, then trees, then another.
Ice shanties hunker down,
haystacks in a dark field.
I've heard that folks
used to move whole houses on skids
across Michigan's lakes
with old diesel trucks or 40's Pontiacs.
Maybe it was colder back then, though tonight,
below zero, it's as good as any winter
old people remember.
I can't understand ice fishermen:
walking out
calm as solid earth,
to auger out a hole,
sit on a milk crate hunched over a line
in red and black plaid,
warming their hands
on hot coffee from the Coleman stove,
swigging beer in the shanty with pals
they've fished with since childhood.
Slime and fish scales
on numb hands as they tug the hook loose
from the hard mouth of a fish.
I've handled fish
caught on a canoe trip,
or the koi from my backyard pond,
the body solid thrashing muscle.
I can't imagine walking out on that surface,
knowing the void underneath.
Some of them still fish in spring
when the rains come
and water puddles on the ice,
bubbles rise.

Infrastructure

A wrecking ball
swings like an anchor
through the hot air
of a summer afternoon,
swings along the side
of a thunderhead
whose prow is edged with light.
City traffic floods
through narrow streets.
The diesel engine chugs
its capstan chant,
and the anchor rises
dripping bricks and plaster dust.

Cranes rise angular above the
debris, lifting fallen girders.
Engines chatter; flakes of
gray-white ash swirl to a
horizon of indifferent blue,
sift under jerry-rigged tarps.
K-9 dogs nose the broken walls and floors,
mounds of stone and steel.

Sanctuary.
Cranes fly in,
dip their graceful landing gear,
extend their wings with a great
flapping, and settle in the marsh.
Gatherings of birds appear on the
horizon, an almost
invisible misty spot that grows,
becomes audible,
jabbering of a thousand birds.

Star-nosed Mole

for Larry Pike

Afterward, God imagined a mole:
snatch of dark fur,
pale polyp flower of a nose
snuffling through the dirt.
Imagined her passing through
like the needle of a blind tailor
turning hems by touch.
Imagined the shovel claws, scraping
toward the knot of black roots,
the ears, deep in the skull,
listening for small movements,
the eyes, no more
than stitches in a shroud.
Even now, all these years later,
the light of her star
gleams down the long tunnels.

Canto Extraño

¿Cómo ir, cómo hablar
con ésta voz extranjera?
¿cómo cantar?
sobre el ruido de las calles.
How to move forward, to speak,
in this strange voice; to sing
above the noise of the streets.

Cuando mis padres vinieron a nuestras calles,
mi lengua era extraña a sus oidos. Me dan
mi lengua con dolor; no tiene raíces.
Olvidan sus lenguas de niñez.
When my parents came to our streets,
they did not speak my language.
They forgot the languages of childhood.

¿Cómo andar en las calles de piedras
con la gente, empresa y amor,
con los niños hermosos
jugando bajo las mesas del mercado,
con sus ojos negros? Y me siento extranjera,
mi canción me parece
la voz extraña de forastera.
Walking in the stone streets
among the people, commerce and love,
the beautiful children
playing under the tables of the market,
their dark eyes. I feel myself a foreigner

(it sings to me
through the fog of my incomprehension;
reading it, even a little, feels like a miracle).
The voice of my first Spanish poem,
the voice of a stranger
(wanting to be invisible, a native,
wanting it also in the U.S.,
far from this other America,
so that I said to a friend that I "pass").

The Spanish burned the Aztec codices.
"¡Ojala!" say the Mexicans—"Allah willing,"
a fragment of Moorish potsherd.
In their faces,
five hundred years.
In mine, only two generations.
Burned tongues I never learned:
the Yiddish of immigrant grandparents,
the Hebrew of the prayerbook, a barred iron gate,
useable only for things
I didn't want to say.

They gave me my tongue with pain (the silence,
if I forget thee, O Jerusalem).
>   *Aqui, no se puede olvidar.*
>   *La voz halla su raíz en las piedras.*
Here, you cannot forget.
The voice finds its roots in the stones.

Diaspora

—noun—

1. A woman with a kerchief over her hair sits on a suitcase. Somewhere, going somewhere else.

2. Distance. The idea of homecoming. Were we taken, or did we go?

3. The smells of cooking hover in the stairwells. The roof leaks.

4. Suburbia.

5. In each generation, scattered like dandelion fluff, the tiny parachute that takes the seed to a place where it might root. The dandelion has a deep taproot. It does not want to move again.

6. When we visit the "old country," we carry phrasebooks and maps of the sacred places.

7. In the book *Nomadic Furniture,* everything folds up or is disposable. Armchairs made of corrugated cardboard, air mattresses.

8. *Mitzvah*-mobiles: backpacks, valises, tents, the movable sanctuary, the Ark with its carrying poles.

9. Don't buy too many books.

Glossary

Adam v adamah: Hebrew. A rabbinic pun. Adam was the first man, made of earth. Adamah is Hebrew for earth or soil.

Arbeit Macht Frei: German. "Work makes (you) free." Written over the gates of a number of concentration camps, including Auschwitz and Dachau.

Burgomeister: German. The chief magistrate of a German city.

Canto Extraño: Spanish. All the Spanish in the poem except the title is contained in the English. Canto is a song. Extraño means "strange"; extranjera means "stranger" or "foreigner."
But the verb extrañar means "to miss" or "to yearn for." Therefore Canto Extraño is a pun, both "Strange/Foreign/Exotic Song" and "Song of Yearning."

Cholent: Yiddish. A hot dish of meat and fruit or beans, traditionally prepared before Sabbath and kept hot for Sabbath meals.

El Imperio: Spanish. Empire.

Erev Yom Kippur: Hebrew. Yom Kippur is the Jewish Day of Atonement and communal confession. The night (erev) which begins the holiday is popularly called Kol Nidre, the name of the All Vows prayer, sung in Aramaic, in which people ask to be forgiven for breaking vows. The melody is the source material for well-known classical cello music composed by Max Bruch.

Fleishig: Yiddish. Meat or flesh. Meat products must be served separately from milk products under the Kosher laws.

Gemütlichkeit: German. A situation encouraging feelings of peacefulness, cheeriness, coziness and social acceptance.

Golem: Hebrew. In Jewish folklore, an artificial man created out of clay and brought to life by writing God's name on its forehead.

Goyim: Yiddish/Hebrew. Gentiles. In Yiddish, pejorative. The Hebrew means literally "the nations."

Haftorah: Hebrew. The portions of the Biblical Prophets read with portions of the Torah, especially on the Sabbath. Students traditionally learn to chant Haftorah for their bar mitzvahs.

Halacha: Hebrew. Usually translated as "Jewish Law," the word is rooted in the idea of "a way of walking."

Hermosa y dilapidada: Spanish. Beautiful and dilapidated.

Klezmer: Yiddish. Eastern European Jewish music played by a small band, often including a fiddle and clarinet.

Kol Nidre: See also *Erev Yom Kippur.*

Konditorei: German. A pastry shop/café.

Malecón: Spanish. Seawall or seafront, often with a seaside drive. In Latin America, usually the drive itself.

Mehitzah: Hebrew. A screen or curtain between men and women in an Orthodox synagogue.

Midrash: Hebrew. A tradition of elaborating, filling gaps or resolving contradictions in texts, especially Torah. Rabbinic midrashim are found throughout the Talmud.

Mikveh: Hebrew. Ritual bath. Both men and women bathe in the mikveh when they are ritually impure (menstruating, noctural emissions, touching a corpse, giving birth are all possible sources of impurity). Converts also use the mikveh before the conversion ceremony. Mikveh water is supposed to come from a natural, free-running source such as rainwater or a stream.

Mitzvah-mobile: Hebrew/English. A "synagogue on wheels" operated by the Chabad Movement of the Lubavitch Hassidim as part of its outreach to non-observant Jews. A mitzvah is a deed commanded in the Torah; in English it has come to mean a good deed.

Pareve: Yiddish/Hebrew. Food that can be eaten with anthing else, without limitations, such as grain, fruit, vegetables and fish. (Special limitations apply to grain products at Passover.)

Patria o muerte: Spanish. Fatherland or death.

Shabbat: Hebrew. Sabbath.

Shiva: Hebrew. The traditional mourning period, seven days, when visitors bring food, sit with mourners, and form a *minyan,* a quorum of 10 Jewish men, to say Kaddish, the prayer for the dead. Derived for the word for the number seven.

Shul: Yiddish. School or synagogue.

Sukkot: Hebrew. Harvest festival, celebrated by building a "booth" (sukkah) with a permeable roof, in which the family and guests are commanded to "dwell," eating festive meals and sometimes sleeping there.

Yahrzeit: Yiddish. The anniversary of a death. A 24-hour candle is traditionally burned in the homes of close family members.

Yalta: mentioned a few times in the Babylonian Talmud as the wife of Rabbi Nachman and implicitly a legal scholar in her own right.

Yeshiva: Hebrew. An institution for the study of Jewish sacred texts, especially Torah and Talmud.

ABOUT THE AUTHOR

Judith Kerman has published eight collections of poetry, most recently *Postcards from America* (Post Traumatic Press), as well as three books of translations of Cuban and Dominican women writers (White Pine Press, BOA Editions, Mayapple Press). She was a Fulbright Scholar in the Dominican Republic in 2002. She founded *Earth's Daughters* magazine in Buffalo, NY (1971 to present) and has run Mayapple Press, located in Woodstock, NY, since 1980. She is Professor of English Emerita from Saginaw Valley State University, where she previously served as Dean of Arts and Behavioral Sciences.

A literary trailer of her poem, "Fragile," and her video documentary about Dominican *Carnaval*, as well as clips of several readings, can be seen on YouTube on the Judith Kerman channel. Visit her website at www.judithkerman.com.